YOUR KNOWLEDGE HAS VALUE

AF149033

- We will publish your bachelor's and master's thesis, essays and papers

- Your own eBook and book -
  sold worldwide in all relevant shops

- Earn money with each sale

Upload your text at www.GRIN.com
and publish for free

Bibliographic information published by the German National Library:

The German National Library lists this publication in the National Bibliography;
detailed bibliographic data are available on the Internet at http://dnb.dnb.de .

Imprint:

Copyright © 2014 GRIN Verlag, Open Publishing GmbH
Print and binding: Books on Demand GmbH, Norderstedt Germany
ISBN: 9783656635499

This book at GRIN:

http://www.grin.com/en/e-book/271538/education-and-employment-status-a-test-
of-the-strong-screening-hypothesis

Yazidu Saidi Mbalamula

Education and Employment Status: A Test of the Strong Screening Hypothesis in Italy

GRIN Publishing

GRIN - Your knowledge has value

Since its foundation in 1998, GRIN has specialized in publishing academic texts by students, college teachers and other academics as e-book and printed book. The website www.grin.com is an ideal platform for presenting term papers, final papers, scientific essays, dissertations and specialist books.

Visit us on the internet:

http://www.grin.com/

http://www.facebook.com/grincom

http://www.twitter.com/grin_com

Title:

Education and Employment Status: A Test of the Strong Screening Hypothesis in Italy

Author (s): Brown, S., & Sessions, J.G.

Year: 1999

Source: Journal of Economics of Education Review/Elsevier

Journal Locus: Number 18; Pg. 397-404

Outline

1. Introduction to Key terms and Concepts
   a. Human Capital Theory
   b. Screening Hypothesis
   c. Employment
      i. Public Employment
      ii. Private Employment
      iii. Self Employment
   d. Statistical Tests Used
      i. Mean
      ii. Standard Deviation
      iii. T-test
      iv. F-test
      v. Chi-Square
2. Summary of the Article/Study
3. Research Design
4. Discussion
   a. Strength (s)
   b. Critic (s)
5. Recommendations
6. Relevancy in Education Settings
7. References

Defining the Key Terms

- **Human Capital Theory** is fundamental theory in the field of Education Economics. This theory expounds that people's learning capacities (education levels) are comparable to other natural resources in the production process. When these capacities are exploited effectively can result into benefits both at enterprise and society levels (Galabawa, 2005; Livingstone, 1997).

- **Screening Hypothesis** is a tentative theory that suggests that inter-educational earnings differentials, even when standardized for differences due to non- educational factors, reflect no direct productivity-enhancing effects of education but only its effects as a device for signaling preexisting ability differences (Layard and Psacharopoulos, 1974).

- **Employment** is a contract between two parties, one being the employer (public or private) and the other being the employee. However, when an individual entirely owns the business for which he or she labors, this is known as *self-employment* (Wikipedia, 2011).

- **Mean** also **Arithmetic mean** as often used in statistics, the term refers to the average of a set of values (i.e., numbers, cars, people e.t.c) or distribution (i.e., ge range, financial income). As well as statistics, means are often used in geometry and analysis (Wikipedia, 2011). The Mean is denoted by X.

- **Standard deviation** is a widely used measure of variability or diversity used in statistics and probability theory. It shows how much variation or "dispersion" there is from the average (mean, or expected value). A low standard deviation indicates that the data points tend to be very close to the mean, whereas high standard deviation indicates that the data points are spread out over a large range of values. This statistic measure is denoted by *SD* (Wikipedia, 2011).

- **T-test** is the most commonly used method to evaluate the differences in means between two groups. For example, the *t*-test can be used to test for a difference in test scores between a group of patients who were given a drug and a control group who received a placebo (Statsoft, 2011).

- **F-test** is any statistical test in which the test statistic has an *F-distribution* under the null hypothesis. It is most often used when comparing statistical models that have been fit to a data set, in order to identify the model that best fits the population from which the data were sampled (Wikipedia, 2011).

- **Chi-square** also referred to as **chi-squared test** or χ^2 **test**, is any statistical hypothesis test in which the sampling distribution of the test statistic is a chi-square distribution when the null hypothesis is true, or any in which this is *asymptotically* true, meaning that the sampling distribution (if the null hypothesis is true) can be made to approximate a chi-square distribution as closely as desired by making the sample size large enough (Wikipedia, 2011).

Summary of the Article

The study presented in the article was comparatively intended to investigate the relationship of two key independent variables, *Education level* (i.e. low, intermediate, high and degree) as related to *Employment status* (i.e. public, private of self employment) on individual earnings. The Human Capital Theory is adopted to contextualize theoretical base of the relationship between the variables.

The theory is further inclined to two strands of Screening hypothesis, Strong Screening Hypothesis (SSH) and Weak Screening Hypothesis (WSH) which in respect contrast, SSH presumes productivity is immutable with schooling used exclusively as a signal, while WSH concedes that not only that primary role of education is to signal, but also it augments inherent productivity. The two opposing theses expand the possibilities beyond Human Capital theorizations.

The study collected data from sample of 1169 individuals (853 employed and 316 self-employed) as derived from Banca d'Italia survey data of 1989 and questionnaires. Two sample selection methods were adopted from Wolpin (1977) and Psacharopoulos (1979), and Bivariate and Multivariate selection methods were employed to control bias on the two resulting dependent variable categories, that is, all employees and self-employed category; and private, public and self employed category. In the same vein, the authors adopted Heckman (1979) bivariate and Lee (1983) sample selection approaches.

The Mincerian function regression analysis was used to treat earnings as products affected by other independent variables, namely age and experience. The results from both analyses (i.e. bivariate and trivariate samples) produced two conclusions which supported both of the two hypotheses (SSH and WSH) in varied contexts of Italy. On the one hand, and in case of supporting WSH, when relative earnings of employees and self-employed were compared, it was observed that the possession of intermediate certificate of University degree significantly

3

raises the earnings for both workers types (i.e. employed and self-employed); also, possession of high school certificate significantly raises the earnings of employed only (see table 1). On the other hand of supporting SSH, where sectoral difference revealed that, public employee accrued higher earnings (SD= 0.420) compared to private sector whose employer maintained albeit relatively low over time, though significant (SD=0.421).

Research Design

The study employed largely Quantitative, but Qualitative methodology was also given considerable account in the data analysis. This observation can be explained by the following observations;

Quantitative Features

- The study intended to determine the cause-effect relationship between the two key variables, which is Education and Employment status and their effect on earnings.
- The study employed several statistical analysis measures to both support and reject the hypotheses (SSH and WSH). Mean, Standard Deviations (SD), T-test, F-test and Chi-square were calculated to establish average, deviation from the average, dispersion, and distribution of effect from education on employment status in support and rejection of the hypotheses developed.
- The study was theory based from Human Capital theory, and the two contrasting hypotheses were derived from this theory.
- The study employed non-experimental design and longitudinal survey design in particular, to study both the effect of education level and employment status on level of individual worker earnings. This required the researchers to account for the two variables inclined against other factors of age, marital status, residence location, nature of job category (i.e. finance, energy e.t.c), whether public or private, or self-employed.
- Control of bias was characteristic feature in screening process of the workers, where bivariate and multivariate standards were adhered.

Qualitative Features

- The statistical analysis bears descriptive analytical reflection in the case of Italy as the study area; for instance, the observations in support of WSH, that education both is for signaling and higher education attainment also results into higher earnings. The authors present the latter situation by reflecting from both Italian government expenditure behavior, which is observed to be averagely higher in primary level and lower in higher education; and also the questionnaires also included items for consumption behaviors for individuals to determine where their earnings were expended, and results showed for those expended in higher certificates and degree, the objective was to signal the quality of their services to their clients.

Strength (s)

The Mincerian regression analysis which was used to estimate earnings was the best approach as it conveniently enables other proxies such as age and work experiences to be accounted for their effect education quality. Consequently, this method enabled researcher to treat earnings as product of other independent variables (Galabawa, 2005).

Also, blending of two adopted analytical methods, bivariate and multivariate, provides sufficient scheme for the such this study whose setting was mediated with variables which required this approach to comprehend the employment mosaic of both employed and self-employment types.

Apart from that, the use of survey design and questionnaires were feasible approaches to conduct a study which involve a large sample in a population, which enables a researcher to reach as many people as possible.

In addition, adoption of the two hypotheses as contrasts to human capital theory, not only provide an opportunity to comprehend the utility of the theory, but also enabled a researcher to extend beyond the limitation of the theory in scrutiny, and thus provide analytical comparison of the two hypotheses, hence substantive description in context of the diverse characteristic study area (Italy).

Moreover, the researchers observed high ethical standard in this study scoring significant credibility of the professionalism. The researchers make account and responsibility over the how data were utilized and not the source (Banca d'Italia), whose involvement should not be considered liable for whatsoever counter-effects, should they happen, of the conclusions made in the study.

5

Lastly but not least, to accommodate unfair and biased comparisons among the study groups, the **control** group has been used to allow avoiding differences that could be attributed to independent variables in the study.

Weakness (es)

Notwithstanding, the two hypotheses give a good account within and beyond the limits of Human capital theory. Nevertheless, attainment of education extends beyond economic and employment benefits, but to long-term benefits such as an appreciation of literature or *cultural capital*. (http://en.wikipedia.org/wiki/Education_economics).

Multi-employment patterns (i.e. full-time, part-time, contract, wage based jobs and combination of these) are not accounted (i.e., person can considerably be public servant but also privately employed, and sometimes self-employed at one or different times) for in determining the earnings differentials,

Recommendations

Given the narrow findings emerging from the study in respect to small area if not only in Italy, there is a need to conduct such study in larger part of Italy and other countries to make the findings more generalizable.

Relevancy

The research study is very useful as it informs the education system on investment choices which also may shade light on specific curricular contents, contexts and delivery modes for particular objectified fields.

Also, such this study is common in educational language studies, where through adoption of Contrastive Analysis Hypothetic (CAH), researchers can analyze the strong and the weak hypothetical scenarios of mastering the particular foreign language in context under study (Brown, 1994).

References

Galabawa, J.C.J. (2005). *Returns to Investment in Education: Startling Revelations and Alternatives before Tanzanians*. Professorial Inaugural Lecture Series No. 45, University of Dar es Salaam. Dar es Salaam. KAD Associates.

Wiersma, W., & Jurs, S.G. (2004). *Research Methods in Education: An Introduction*. China Light Industry Press. Person Education.

Brown, H.D. (1994). *Principles of Language Learning and Teaching*. New Jersey, USA. Tina Cover

YOUR KNOWLEDGE HAS VALUE

- We will publish your bachelor's and master's thesis, essays and papers

- Your own eBook and book - sold worldwide in all relevant shops

- Earn money with each sale

Upload your text at www.GRIN.com and publish for free